IN THE BEGINNING...

The two Ronnies are probably the most successful comedy duo ever to be screened on British TV. Script writer and editor, Peter Vincent says that the joy of writing for them is that you always know you'll get the best possible performance of the words. Of course Ronnie Barker and Ronnie Corbett were not always part of the same act. They met socially for the first time at the Buxton Club behind the Haymarket Theatre. At this time, Ronnie Corbett had done three series of *Crackerjack!* with Eammon Andrews and remembers that the script budget for this show was eight guineas.

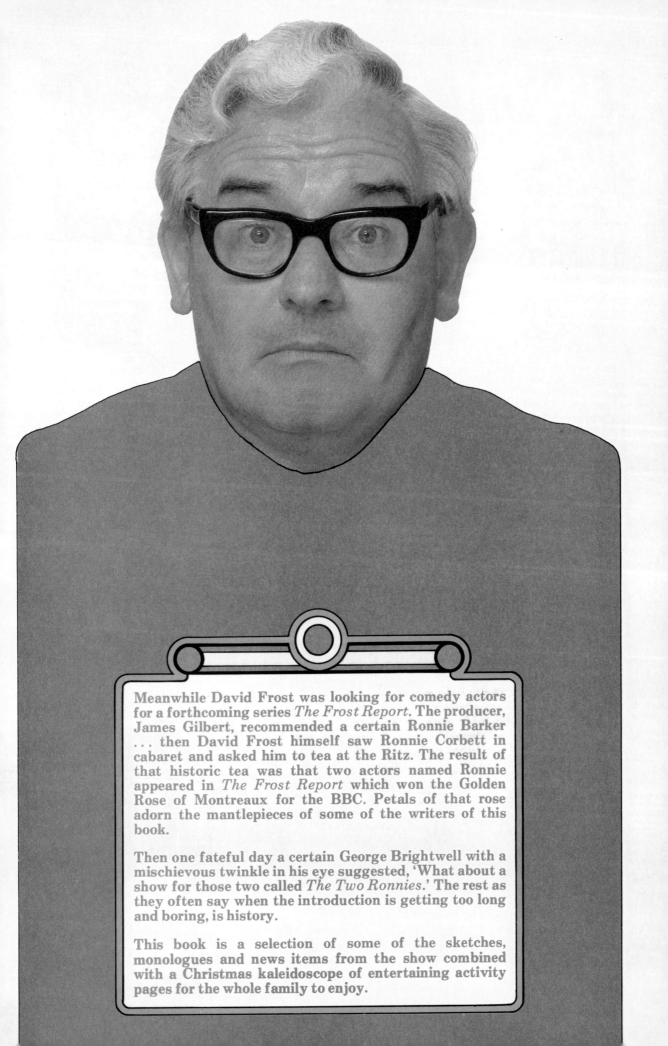

Meanwhile David Frost was looking for comedy actors for a forthcoming series *The Frost Report*. The producer, James Gilbert, recommended a certain Ronnie Barker ... then David Frost himself saw Ronnie Corbett in cabaret and asked him to tea at the Ritz. The result of that historic tea was that two actors named Ronnie appeared in *The Frost Report* which won the Golden Rose of Montreaux for the BBC. Petals of that rose adorn the mantlepieces of some of the writers of this book.

Then one fateful day a certain George Brightwell with a mischievous twinkle in his eye suggested, 'What about a show for those two called *The Two Ronnies*.' The rest as they often say when the introduction is getting too long and boring, is history.

This book is a selection of some of the sketches, monologues and news items from the show combined with a Christmas kaleidoscope of entertaining activity pages for the whole family to enjoy.

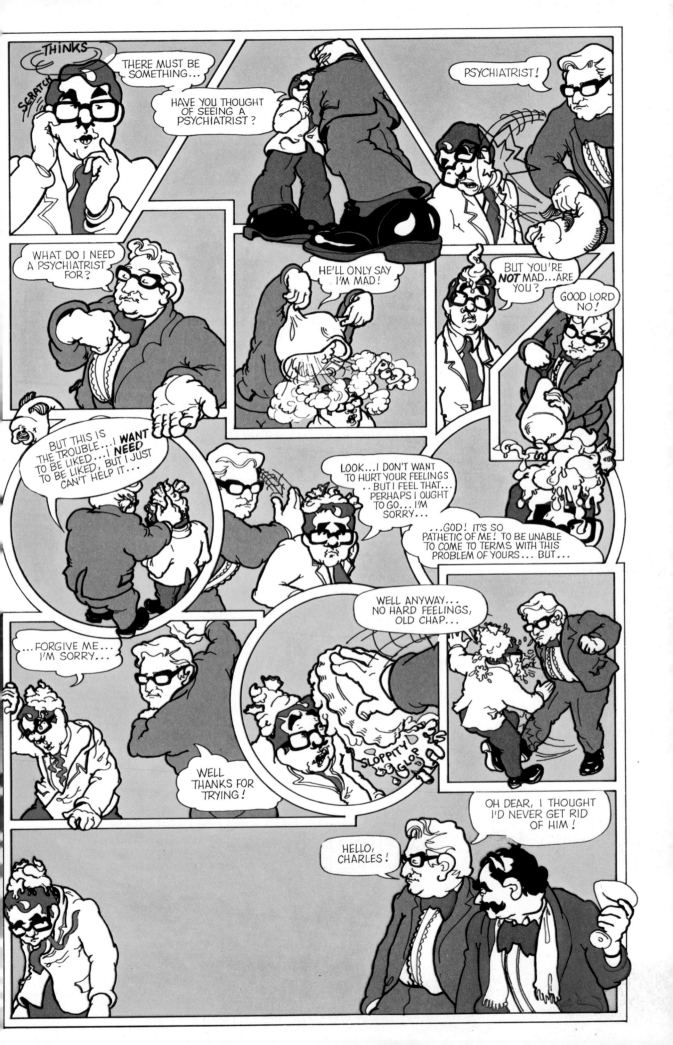

'Last week we tested 12 different kinds of glue. I said that Boffo glue was best, and I'm sticking to it. Now certain people have bandied it about that I favour Boffo products because they pay me. Absolute rubbish! You should be boiled in oil for thinking it . . . And I recommend Boffo oil.

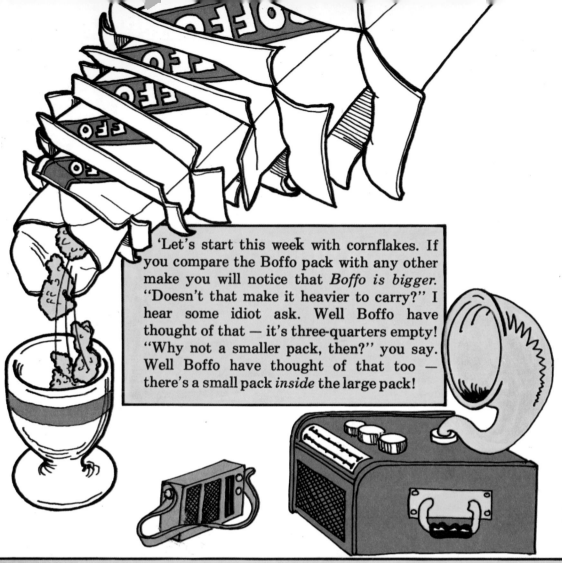

'Let's start this week with cornflakes. If you compare the Boffo pack with any other make you will notice that *Boffo is bigger*. "Doesn't that make it heavier to carry?" I hear some idiot ask. Well Boffo have thought of that — it's three-quarters empty! "Why not a smaller pack, then?" you say. Well Boffo have thought of that too — there's a small pack *inside* the large pack!

'From cornflakes it's but a short step to transistor radios for the pocket. Two new makes this week. One silly little Japanese one the size of a cigarette packet. And this one... And it's British! For my money that's the one. I mean who could possibly lose it?... Let's see who made it... Well, what a coincidence! Yes, Boffo make the world's largest miniature radio. And another important selling point — you can hardly hear it, so no complaints from the neighbours!

'There's no room for bias about foodstuffs as *every* firm must list the contents on the package... Let's take one at random... *Boffo Beef Risotto*... mmmm!... Sounds good... It reads: "Contains beef substitute, vegetable substitute, rice substitute, edible spices, inedible spices, monosodium glutamate substitute, and a rusty nail." Well, you can't be fairer than that! Unless you dye your hair with Boffolene hair dye, or use Boffo hair restorer, as I did on this billiard ball...

'Earlier today I washed two identical shirts — one with *Boffo Blue*, the other with a cheese grater. You might be surprised to learn that while both shirts came out with the same somewhat shredded appearance, the Boffo washed shirt *was* three shades whiter!

'I also made a strictly impartial cooking test — monitored by a neutral observer, the Managing Director of Boffo. I took two different products — a *Boffo Chicken Curry* and a large stone — and cooked each for 20 minutes at gas mark 7. Later, when a Welsh housewife tasted the *Boffo Chicken Curry* she pronounced it "Boffo Chicken Curry" in a Welsh accent. Whereas the large stone even when adorned with chips and peas is still *extremely* tough. See?

'And here's a bit of news: This week every single Boffo product costs 45% less. "45% less than what?" I hear you say. Well, 45% less than it will cost next week.

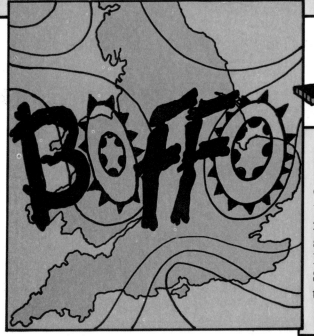

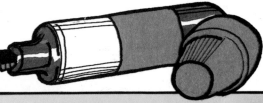

'I'll finish, as always, with our *Shoppers' Weather Guide.* As you can see there are two depressions which have been marked with two O's. But in the midlands it will be fairly foggy which I'll mark with two FF's. And since Western districts will be affected by Hurricane Bertha I'll mark that with a big B. So there it is, BOFFO! It's a good buy from them, and a goodbye from me. Goodbye!'

INTRODUCING

It is almost as hard for me to start this piece — the first of its kind that I've ever attempted — as it would be for Ronnie and I to open the show without these cherished News Items. I am going to prepare myself for the task in the manner of the true writer.

I shall retire to my study — a warm room facing the garden, decorated and carpeted in guardsman's red (see *Brolac colour chart*) with curtains in a bold black and white houndstooth (see David Hicks' *Living with Style*). I am looking out on Surrey heathers and silver birches and *still* wondering how to start. I have around me the paraphernalia of the essayist, a cup of strong, sweet, dark brown coffee (see West Wickham *Cash and Carry*), a pack of half used Kleenex (see Cole Porter's *Song Book*), a signed picture of the Duke of Windsor (signed by my cousin, Bert, that is), and a pack of vivid green Japanese pentels jammed casually into a Dartington glass tankard.

For this one foreword I have spent a fortune in Rymans — three packs of paper in different sizes, all colours of pens, paper clips, bulldog clips, drawing pins, two diaries, a pocket filing system, three reels of Sellotape, two boxes of refills for a pen I don't possess and I am *still* wondering how to start. I put my pen down, finish the coffee and then I have the most marvellous idea. I'll ring Spike Mullins and get him to do it.

These "news items", the pick of all those Ronnie Corbett and I have delivered from behind that double desk, have become such a trade-mark of the show that I cannot imagine starting and finishing in any other way.

Obviously. I remember with affection some of the gags — the elephant doing a ton on the M1; the contortionist who had come from Australia to look up his relatives; and the stunt-man who fell sixty feet, landing on Raquel Welch (his condition was described later as extremely comfortable), but for the most part they had 'flowed away down the dark stream of memory' as Lionel Blair once put it. What a treat, then, to sample them once again in this splendid and rib-tickling selection. I hope you enjoy them as much as I did.

RB
. . . We'll be talking by long distance 'phone to a Scotsman who found an Australian penny and emigrated.

RC
Then we'll be talking to a stereo expert about his favourite breakfast . . .
Two bowls of rice crispies ten feet apart.

RC
Then I'll be demonstrating the latest cooking aid from Africa . . . The non-pan frying stick

RB
And we'll talk to the Texas man who made a fortune selling smokeless fuel to Red Indian couples who are not speaking to each other.

RC
And I'll be telling you about the octopus saved from drowning this week on the Argyllshire coast. A passing piper gave it the kiss of life and three choruses of A Scottish Soldier

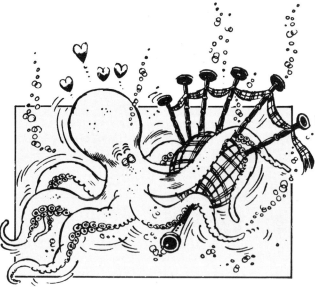

RB
We'll be discussing four new classic series — What Katy did, What Katy did next, Who did what to Katy, and Son of Katy.

RB
We will then talk to a remarkable man who crossed a Rhode Island Red with a waitress and got a chicken that lays tables.

RC
Then he crossed a truss with a polo mint and got a Nutcracker Suite.

RB
And we'll meet a scientist who crossed a lady's hairpiece with a tomcat and a duck and got a plait billed duckypus.

RC
And a lady scientist who crossed the theories of Sigmund Freud with those of Albert Einstein and got sex at the speed of light.

CLUES ACROSS

1 A large African animal.
9 This is the name for someone who takes things away.
11 A shrub with very large flowers.
13 A very, very, **very**, **VERY**, *VERY* long time!
14 To tear something sharply.
16 The Queen is the head of the _____ Family.
18 This one's backwards!
19 When you're furious you can fly into a _____.
20 If you are going on a journey you use a map to work out your _____.
21 The opposite of down.
23 This person works for a newspaper.
26 In America they sometimes call this person a 'rodent exterminator'!
29 This could be the head of a country — or a piece of wood thirty centimetres long!
31 You and me — that's _____.
32 Another word for 'to steal'.
34 Here's a fruit that's delicious in a crumble.
36 Rubbish!
37 If you're travelling by train, let's hope it doesn't go off the _____.
39 Trees have these — but you don't always see them.
41 The most important person in my life, that's _____!
43 'You owe nothing, you see' — try saying that with just five letters!
46 A mechanical man.
47 When you're leaving the house, you're going _____.
49 A short way of saying Public Works Department.
51 This comes before two.
52 If you're not against something, are you _____ it?
53 This army's marching backwards!

CLUES DOWN

1 It's a _____ thing to find two people as funny as the two Ronnies!
2 What you do at the ironing board.
3 A short form of Edward.
4 A washing powder.
5 A fish.
6 She kept Adam company.
7 These are just three letters, but put a W in front of them and you'll have a little bird!
8 This must be obeyed.
10 A short form of Anthony.
12 The Americans call someone who rootoots a _____!
14 What the farmers do at harvest time.
15 A verse.
17 Someone who appears in plays.
19 This is the name of a bear, but it isn't Paddington and it isn't Pooh.
22 A good way of getting to sleep is to count sheep jumping over this.
24 To live you've got to _____.
25 The way a Scotsman says 'Oh!'
27 A fungus you can eat!
28 Parsley is a _____. So are basil and sage and thyme.
29 Rugby Union Rules — for short.
30 An oar in a muddle!
33 _____ roses are wild roses.
35 Where you put the carpet.
38 To bend over.
40 What the Americans call the Underground.
42 Another way of saying 'Come in!'
44 A fish.
45 What covers a house.
48 The United Nations Organisation — for short.
50 The Two Ronnies' favourite drink!

AMAZE YOUR FRIENDS!

Start from either end and find your way to the centre.

SKETCHERISM SPOON

One of the special features of The Two Rons is Ronnie Barker's skill with words. Every keen schoolperson will remember that best-known spoonerism specimen — 'Kingquering congs their titles take.' But for the millions who don't . . .

'Good Evening. The Spoonerism. *Of Men and Words* deals with a man who was born July 22, 1844. The Reverend William Archibald Spooner of New College, Oxford . . . the man who committed such inadvertent transpositions as — 'Yes indeed, the Lord *is* a shoving leopard,' and the immortal Royal toast: 'To the queer old Dean!'

'A new play opening next week deals with the home life of the Spoon who invented the mannerism . . . er . . . man who invented the Spoonerism! Here, in the opening scene of the play, we see the players representing The Reverend Spooner himself and his worthy wife:

'Ah, there you are,' *said she,* 'Beautiful day isn't it?'

'Quite so,' *came the Reverend Father's instant retort,* 'The shine is sunning, the chirds are burping . . . lovers are killing and booing . . . It makes one glide to be a lav!'

'It's just as well you're in a good mood,' *quoth she as she gave him his shirt,* 'Because look what the laundry did to your best shirt!' *Staring incredulously, Spooner exclaimed,* 'Good heavens they've freed the slaves!'

'Frayed the sleeves, dear,' *his ever patient wife consoled.*

'I did that, saidn't I?'

She ignored this further complication and moved on (a course which had proved advisable more than once before). 'They've also torn the collar and smashed all the buttons . . .'

Looking closer, the great man replied, 'Quite so! It never pains but it roars. Button, collar and sleeves at one swell foop! Well I'll fight them nooth and tail! Naith and tool! I'll go down and smith them to shmashereens.' *Making for the door, he concluded:* 'I'm going to tump into a jaxi!'

SPETCHEROON SKISM

'William, wait!' *advised the good lady,* 'Surely such a scene would be unseemly for a man of your calling?'

Spinning round, her husband took careful stock, 'You're quite right my dear. After all, I *am* a clan of the moth. Better to let sleeping logs die. To hue is ermine . . .' *And so saying he returned to his seat.*

'That's better,' *his wife whispered in her conciliatory way,* 'Do you feel like some breakfast?'

'Indood I dee!' *Spooner replied,* 'A suggestion to warm the heartles of my _ _ _ whoops! . . . cockles of my heart. I rather fancy some hot toatered bust, a rasher of strakey beacon, and some of the cereal that goes pap, snockle and crap!'

Blanching at the suggestion, his good wife swallowed hard and said: 'Very well, William. And while you're eating it, I shall be packing my trunk.'

'Tracking your punk!' *he exclaimed.*

'Yes, William,' *she replied with uncustomary fortitude,* 'You see, I'm leaving you.'

'Leaving me after 20 years of bedded wiss?' *he parried with a nervous laugh,* 'This must be some rather jathetic poke. You can't mean suddenly to destroy my entire lay of wife!'

'I'm quite serious, William,' *came the calmly considered reply.* 'I'm leaving you.'

'But my dear,' *he rejoined,* 'Consider the word of the Highly Boble: "What God Hath joined together, let no son put Amanda." Er . . . "Let no pan soot amunder" . . . Dear me, I'm getting my tang all tungled!'

'Exactly, *that's* why I'm leaving you.'

'What *do* you mean?' *Spooner fixed his eyes unerringly on hers.*

'It's quite simple,' *she said,* 'I can't spoon any more Standerisms!'

For a brief moment she stood stunned by what she had said. Then gathering her skirts about her, she ran shrilly screaming from the room . . .

FINIS

Menu

Frewed stuit
Flan brakes
Pot horridge
Juit fruces
Wedded shreet

———

Killed grippers
Strakey beacon

Eggs:
Froad, bieled or poiched

———

Hot toatered bust

TRICKS &

When your stomach's extended by the Christmas turkey, what better way to spend the time than extending your mind still further? See the last page for solutions. No cheating!

PICTURE PUZZLES

A. In the diagram below, A and B represent 2 islands around which a river runs. As you can see there are 15 bridges across this river. Can you pass in turn over all these bridges without passing over the same bridge twice?

B. How many animals can you see in this wood, and what are they?

THERE ARE MORE THINGS IN HEAVEN AND EARTH . . .

If you do not believe in ghosts, then this is a game for you. In a good light, look steadily for 30 seconds at the cross in the eye of the skull below. Then fix your gaze on a wall, ceiling, or blank sheet of paper for another 30 seconds. Do you still not believe in ghosts?

PICK YOUR BRAINS

1. Simple when you know how. Arrange 16 tooth picks in the position shown below.

Now, see if you can re-arrange just 3 of the picks to form 4 complete squares.

2. Here's a simpler problem, or is it? Arrange 24 tooth picks to form 9 squares as shown. Can you remove just 8 picks so that only 2 squares are left on the table?

3. Now this does need some practice. Once you have mastered it we reckon you can safely bet your Dad an extra week's pocket money that he cannot do it! Take 5 tooth picks and bend each of them into a V-

PUZZLES

shape. Place them together on a smooth surface and without touching them see if you can transform the shape they make into a 5-pointed star. A useful clue — you will need a drop of water and the picks must be wooden.

4. For this you'll need an empty bottle, a wooden tooth pick and a 1/2 p piece. Break the pick almost in half and place it and the coin on the bottle, as shown in the picture. Can you make the coin fall into the bottle without touching it?

5. Finally, can you build a bridge between 3 wine glasses using just 3 wooden tooth picks? It must be solid enough to support a 4th glass.

An illusion you might call 'walking the goose'. Place the edge of a card (your Dad's business card would be good) on the dotted line. Then drop your face towards the edge of the card and you will see the goose move towards the sugar!

DOING THE IMPOSSIBLE WITH DOMINOES

This makes card castles look easy. Can you balance a complete set of dominoes on one piece that stands upright? A useful tip — build the horizontal sections separately and lift ever so carefully into place.

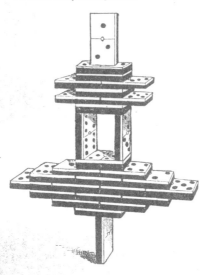

SCIENCE AT PLAY

If you have successfully done all the above tricks, try this one superkid! Set a stool, as is shown in the diagram below, about 9 or 10 inches away from the wall. Plant your feet well away from it and clasp the stool firmly with both hands. Rest your head against the wall, lift the stool and then try, without moving your feet, to stand upright.

MAC TOURISM

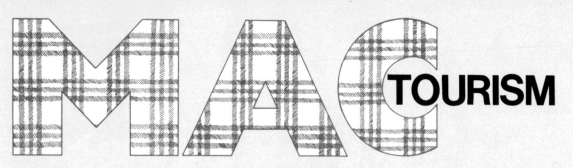

If, like most families confined like bears in a cage by the Yuletide freeze, you are looking forward to your summer hols, look no further than Ronnie Barker's (alias Wee Willie McGorbals) salute to the Scottish tourist industry.

Should sensitive Sassenachs detect more than a smattering of partiality in our presenter (or if you think he's downright rude!) remember that Wee Willie McGorbals comes from Scotland, and like a great many of his countrymen, cannot help it . . .

'Good evening, Hullo, Scots wae, and up your haggis. I'm Scottish by the way. My name is Wee Willie McGorbals of the clan McGorbals . . . *especially* after the operation. I am *P*resident of the *I*nstitute of *S*cottish *T*ourism. In short I'm P.I.S.T.

'Now, how do you get There? Well, let's look at the map . . .

'Take the old fashioned scenic route, over the Braes of Altnasporran by way of the Quilt of Skelt, to the Kyles of Bute, where old Angus McFergus will row you across in his old Gaelic skiff (if he's not out flashing his sporran or waving his wee caber down at the Cock-a-Leekie Inn with Inverness Lil).

'Then why not take the road to the Isles? You go by way of Bannockburn . . . (where in 1314 the patriot Robert the Bruce and his gallant clans routed the treacherous lecherous English rabble who were sent to pillage their native homelands) — But let bygones be bygones and you'll be assured of a great welcome at the Bannockburn Inn, where you can stand by the fire and sorely burn your bannocks! Drive on by the sodden fields of Flodden and Culloden (where the gallant Bonnie Prince Charlie's troops were brutally massacred by the cursed Earl of Cumberland and his gangs of illiterate drunken murderous English thugs . . . ahem!).

'There's a very nice souvenir shop on the battlefield where you can buy Dr. Hamish Kinley's book of Scottish portraits known as Dr. Kinley's Facebook. This book is full of people not generally known as Scottish such as the great road makers, Macadam and Maceve. You know the old Scottish story.

pictures to prove it. Here's the great Scottish composer Ludwig McBeethoven.

And here's the Mona McLisa.

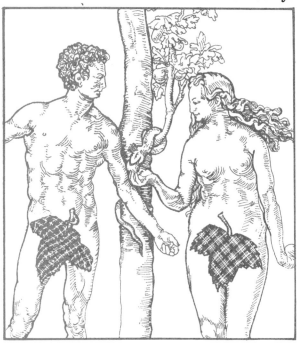

He said: "Here's an apple, Maceve" and she said: "Ta, Macadam'. There's the inventor of radio spaghetti, Macaroni, who also invented McTurtle soup, and the famous Celtic murderer Jock the Ripper; the inventor of dentistry, Phil McAvity, and Ben Doon, the Scottish pouffe. It's true, here are some

'Now, if you drive round this forty mile long stag, blocking the road here, you'll find nary hoose nor moose nor goose for close on a hundred miles, and why? Because the grasping greedy grouse-shooting English landlords burned out the honest crofters so that half-witted English chinless wonders could massacre the innocent Scottish birds.

'Speaking of Scottish birds, visit the birthplace of lovely Flora MacDonald, the flower of the Hebrides and Flora MacDougall, the self raising flower. And if you fancy some highland sports, she's one — or if you fancy a tartan troos, she's one. And what's the price that never varies? That's MacDougall's too.

'If you meet with hostility once in a while it's only because you Sassenach footpads have plundered us for ten centuries and now tax our goodly Scottish oil, leaving us mortgaged to the kilt — God rot the English! May they never get tickets to see Scotland in the World Cup when they haven't even reached the last sixteen!'

At this point our recording broke down. Wee Willie's fury was reflected in his picking up his bagpipes and hurling them into the air. Eventual calm was heralded by the sound of breaking glass and dying bagpipe noises as they fell to the ground. Pulling himself together as best he could, Wee Willie continued:

'So, occasionally when you ask for a wee dram of whisky, you might get given a glass of Rory MacDonald's Revenge; one part of distilled ptarmigan, which as you can see begins with a 'p' (and so would you if you were being distilled), and one part stagnant bogwater strained in the Trossachs, which is sorely painful . . .

'Well that's Scotland for the noo the noo the noo, and that is the end of the noos. Next week my colleague Even Up Evan Up Jenkins . . . of Wales . . . will tell you of the lovely Welsh hills, where you can roam at peace all day without seeing a soul, and why? Because the filthy English invaders plundered and ravished and raped the fair sod of Wales. Nice to see you all — and good McNight.'

But First the News...

RB
Here is the news. The pound had another good day yesterday. It rose sharply at ten o'clock, had a light breakfast, and went for a stroll in the park.

RB
And shares fell 36 points when the Bank of England announced a closing down sale.

RC
This contrasts with last week when the pound closed at only 2.4 against the Matabele Gumbo Bead.

RC
Another accident occurred today, this time in a Hollywood Bowling Alley, when Telly Savalas bent down to do up a shoelace and a passer-by stuck two fingers up his nostrils.

RB
And the Chancellor has announced new plans for shortening the dole queues. He's asking the men to stand closer together.

RB
The longest ever swearing-in of a witness ended in the High Court this afternoon after 6½ days when the witness, Bert Osby, instead of holding the Bible and reading out the card, held the card and read out the Bible.

RC
The title of most considerate father of the year goes to Mr. Clarence Larkin of Stroud. He put a silencer on his shot gun because his daughter wanted a quiet wedding.

RB
Whilst at home, there was consternation in Downing Street when one of Denis Healey's eyebrows was indecently assaulted by a hedgehog.

RC
However, in a white paper today the Government revealed plans for the small shopkeeper . . .

A lower counter.

and Over to our Sports Desk...

RB
Soccer violence. Fighting between Rovers and United fans tonight was interrupted for ninety minutes when the pitch was invaded by twenty-two players.

RC
Whilst, at the combined Highland Games and Vegetable show held today, Mr Hamish MacGillivray set a new record of 226 feet in the salad-tossing event.

RC
Reports that athletes indulge in too much sex before meetings were hotly denied by sprinter Wellesley Blunt. He went on to win the hundred metres in a time of two hours thirty-seven minutes.

RB
And last night, a publican sacked all his topless barmaids for dipping into the till.

RB
Les Grout, the only man ever to play in an all Ladies Soccer team said tonight that he was very happy after his first week with his new club. He scored three times this evening . . . Once in the match and twice in the showers!

RC
The giant worm failed to mate yet again at London Zoo today. Its rear end had a headache.

Water is a refreshing or unrefreshing fact of our climate depending upon the season. Television pictures of anguished ladies with large receptacles queueing beside solitary taps on village greens appear in dreary conflict with pictures of anguished ladies watching their worldly goods floating down the high street in four feet of flood water. Thus it behoves us to remember that deep down in the catacombs of Whitehall we have a representative responsible for our needs in such times of national crisis . . .

WATER

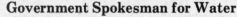

Government Spokesman for Water

Note the slicked down hair, the thin municipal moustache, the air of complete confidence that he at least earns every last penny of our taxes apportioned to his worthy task.

'Good evening. I want to speak to you tonight about the water shortage. Now there have been rumours that the Government are washing their hands of the whole problem. But we're not, since there isn't any water!

'My job is to be positive, so let's deal straight away with this ridiculous rumour that cows in the North East are producing dried milk.

'It's true!

'Nor is this an isolated case. Here's a chart of Britain's goldfish reserves which shows without a shadow of doubt that they have been left high and dry — yes, very dry and extremely high.

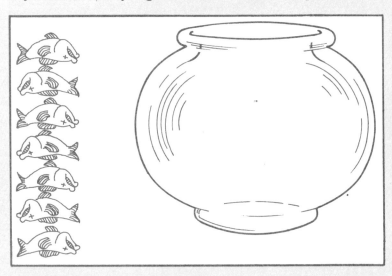

'And it's true that in the annual Upper Thames fishing contest yesterday, the winner caught a seven pound ferret. Which in turn brings me to sport . . .

'The water shortage is going to affect sport just a bit. Next week there's going to be treacle skiing at Ruislip; the Fifth Test will be at Henley and the Boat Race will be at Wimbledon closely followed by caber-tossing and swan-upping (though not necessarily in that order). At Ascot, the water will only be turned on on Ladies Day and the ladies will be turned on on Water Day.

'But what are the Government *doing*?

'Well here's a map which makes it all simple . . .

'And here's the *real* map which makes it look a ghastly mess . . .

'But what can *you* do about it?

'Firstly you can buy our new economy watering can . . .

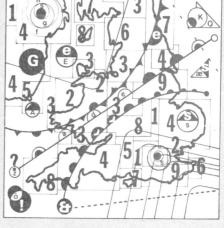

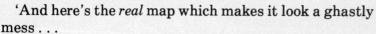

'And you know we really can't have everyone washing their cars down on Sundays. Do it on Wednesdays.

'Try to combine going to the toilet with cleaning the windows.

'And how about making tea without water? Well, here's a teapot. Put in one spoonful per person and one for the pot and pour yourselves a nice cup of tealeaves.

'I have to end with an emergency message for girls in the London area. From now on you're asked to share your baths, since the only bathroom to have continuous water will be at Buckingham Palace. Or, to sum up, it's either two pairs or a Royal Straight Flush.

'Goodnight!'

Your 1980 H

ARIES
March 21 — April 20

Arian people are assertive and pushy but need to be loved. Congratulations! 1980 could be your year. You suddenly become the most popular person in your street — you move to another town!

TAURUS
April 21 — May 21

A year of mixed fortunes. There's good news and bad news. The good news is that you enter a competition and win £10,000. The bad news is that you get paid £1 a year for the next 10,000 years.

GEMINI
May 22 — June 21

As the first of the Air Signs you have an insatiable desire to explore all of every part of life. But look out! Your stars predict that you will fall off a stepladder, get run over by a steamroller, be bitten by a rabid dog, accidentally burn down your house and acquire a severe case of mongolian swamp fever . . . and the day after looks just as bad.

CANCER
June 22 — July 23

Cancer is the Water sign and you start the year full of energy — until you accidentally stick a wet finger into an electric light socket!

LEO
July 24 — August 23

Born under the fifth sign of the Zodiac and ruled by the Sun, you are big and round and sunny. If you have a friend who is a Cancerean then take him along to the local Youth Club. The word is that someone shoves a live crab down the back of your trousers and you win first prize in the annual disco-dancing championships!

VIRGO
August 24 — September 23

You share your sign with such famous people as Marlene Dietrich, Edward Kennedy, Winston Churchill and Leo Tolstoy. And 1980 could be a great year for you. You certainly start it off on the right foot as somebody saws off your left one!

rror Scope!

LIBRA
September 24 — October 23

Librans are ruled by the planet Venus. Venus is a planet that demands harmony, beauty, artistry. And it's good news for Librans in 1980 as from this year you will never have to visit the dentist again — all your teeth will drop out.

SCORPIO
October 24 — November 22

Your Star Sign indicates that you are going on a long journey later in the year. You will travel to a far distant land where you will meet a tall dark stranger. He will eat you.

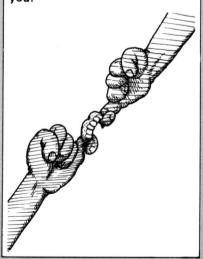

SAGITTARIUS
November 23 — December 21

Being ruled by the planet Jupiter you are prone to being over-buoyant. In 1980 you rise meteorically to the top of your class — your own fault for messing about with matches in the Chemistry Lab!

CAPRICORN
December 22 — January 20

Old Chinese proverb says, 'The ambitious goat climbs slowly up the mountainside.' New interests and activities are indicated for 1980. You will take up Yoga but develop lumbago and find it difficult to make ends meet.

AQUARIUS
January 21 — February 19

1980 is a year in which you will remain true to your sign. Ruled as you are by the Planet Uranus you enjoy revolutionary untraditional things. And this year you will break the three-minute mile due to your tie being caught on the handlebars of a passing 650 cc motor bike.

PISCES
February 20 — March 20

Positive Neptune gives the power associated with Pisces — sensitivity. And although this year sees you mature into a fully responsible member of society, there is one overbearing emotional upset when somebody sinks your rubber duck!

BEHIND THE SCENES

Hello, my name is Eric T. Budge and I'm about to take you on a flying visit round a typical TV Studio. Children are the world's biggest TV gapers — the average British child watches 24 hours of TV every week — but I wonder how many of you know what goes on behind the scenes.

Above you can see actors playing their parts, cameramen shooting the scene according to a pre-arranged plan, lighting experts helping create the atmosphere, and sound controllers directing the microphone boom at the sound source, always making sure the boom is 'out-of-shot'.

Above you can see the sound control room where a sound supervisor and engineers control the sound reproduction.

Everyone on the studio floor is controlled by the producer sitting high above them in a small room. Below you can see him watching a stack of TV screens that show what every camera 'sees'. He selects which shot you see at home by telling a vision mixer to 'cut' abruptly from one shot to the next or 'mix' one camera view gradually into another. Besides a technical liaison manager and some assistants there's a vision operator who keeps constant watch on the signal levels produced by the cameras.

The Control Room set high above the Studio floor is the centre of all activity.

Before the production team can set to work, writers will work out the final script with the producer and script editor. Then the producer will discuss the set with the designer. And the casting director will audition actors to play the parts.

Well, that's it for a lightning visit, although there can be many more people helping create a TV production. Here you can see a typical group, some we have seen in action and others too often taken for granted.

There are set designers, carpenters, scene setters, stage hands, painters, researchers, editors, writers, wardrobe and props staff, make-up artists, directors . . .

Producers, cameramen, engineers, electricians, lighting and sound staff, prompters, control room staff . . .

Actors, musicians, conductors . . .

Could you work in TV?

As the production approaches, properties staff gather together every item you will see on the set, wardrobe staff supply or tailor costumes for the actors, and make-up artists help mould their characters or simply prepare them for the powerful TV lights.

EURO CHRISTMAS

GOOD EVENING, BON NUIT, GUTEN ABEND!

NOW WE ARE IN EUROPE, IT'S BEEN DECIDED THAT THIS IS THE LAST XMAS TO BE SPENT IN THE OLD ENGLISH MANNER!

AS FROM NEXT YEAR, DUE TO AN **EEC** AGREEMENT, CHRISTMAS WILL BECOME **EURO-CHRISTMAS!**

WE'LL BE LINKING HANDS ACROSS THE SEA. WHAT WILL THIS MEAN? WELL IT WON'T BE EASY.

IT WILL BE A TIME OF CLOSED FACTORIES AND NON-PRODUCTIVITY, WHEN THE TIDE OF THE NEW TECHNOLOGICAL MIRACLE IS TURNED OFF, LIKE AN EMPTY BUCKET...

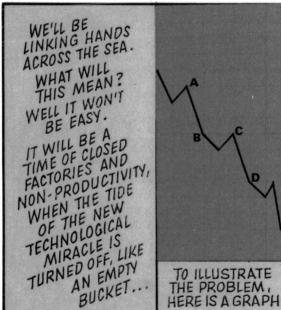

TO ILLUSTRATE THE PROBLEM, HERE IS A GRAPH

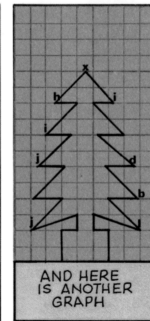

AND HERE IS ANOTHER GRAPH

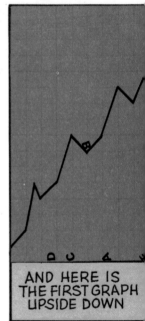

AND HERE IS THE FIRST GRAPH UPSIDE DOWN

HERE ARE SOME HANDS ACROSS THE SEA!

AND HERE IS AN EMPTY BUCKET. BUT THINGS WON'T BE AS BAD AS THAT! WHAT WILL EURO-CHRISTMAS BE LIKE? WELL, YOU WON'T BE ALLOWED TURKEY, BECAUSE TURKEY ISN'T A MEMBER OF THE COMMON MARKET...

YOU'LL HAVE TO ROAST WEST GERMANY INSTEAD, WITH BRUSSEL SPROUTS. FOLLOWED BY EURO-CHRISTMAS PUDDING, OR EUROPUDDING

NOW, AFTER YOUR XMAS DINNER, YOU WILL ALL PULL YOUR EUROPEAN CRACKERS—PROVIDED YOU'VE FINISHED WITH YOUR PUDDING. HERE IS THE NEW 7-STAGE EUROCRACKER. OH DEAR... THE ITALIAN STAGE FAILED!

NOW HERE'S NEXT YEAR'S EUROJOKE:

'MEIN DACHSHUND HAST NO HOOTER!' 'HOW DOES HE GESMELLEN?' 'TERRIBLE!'

NOW IN THE LARGER EUROPE, WE CAN'T ALL HAVE XMAS AT ONCE. WE'D BE TOO VULNERABLE TO A HOSTILE POWER WHEN EVERYBODY'S PULLING WISHBONES, WEARING SWEATERS 3 SIZES TOO SMALL, AND CLIMBING DOWN CHIMNEYS STONED TO THE EYEBALLS!

SO, **XMAS** WILL BE **STAGGERED.** IN FUTURE, EVERY DAY WILL BE XMAS DAY. **SOMEWHERE.** FOR BRITAIN, XMAS WILL START AS USUAL IN OCTOBER

ONLY 355 SHOPPING DAYS TO XMAS

FRANCE WILL HAVE XMAS ON MARCH 9TH. DENMARK ON APRIL 18TH. LUXEMBOURG, DUE TO A COMPUTER ERROR, ON AUGUST **86**TH! WALES WILL CELEBRATE XMAS WITH THE JEWISH NEW YEAR. AND WE'LL CONTINUE TO IGNORE SCOTLAND ...

NOW IF ALL THAT SOUNDS COMPLICATED, HERE IS AN EASY GUIDE :

HOLLAND WILL HAVE A WHOLE YEAR OF XMASES IN 1980, DUE TO A STATISTICAL FREAK WHO WORKS IN THE OFFICE HERE.

AND GERMANY WON'T HAVE ANY XMASES UNTIL 1998 — SERVES YOU RIGHT YOU SILLY OLD KRAUTS !

DOLE

SPRACHEN HERE

IF YOU WISH TO VISIT OTHER AREAS DURING **THEIR** XMAS, YOU'LL HAVE TO OBTAIN A PERMIT FROM THE **STATIONERY** OFFICE. THIS IS TO **STOP** PEOPLE WITH CARAVANS HAVING XMAS ALL YEAR ROUND

FLIGHTS TO HOLLAND →

THIRDLY, AND LASTLY, YOU MUST DO UP YOUR PRESENTS IN THE EUROPEAN GIFT-WRAPPING PAPER— **EUROPAPER**— OR YOU'LL BE SHOT!

IT SHOWS AN **ITALIAN** WAITER STUFFING A **FRENCH** ONION INTO A **DANISH** PASTRY— WATCHED BY PRINCESS GRACE OF **MONACO**...

AND ON THE BACK IT'S THE OTHER WAY ROUND

SPECIAL STAMPS WILL BE ISSUED, RETAINING THE XMAS SPIRIT WITH THE QUEEN'S HEAD IN ONE CORNER AND THE PARSON'S NOSE IN THE OTHER

WELL, THAT JUST ABOUT WRAPS IT UP. AND IF IT DOESN'T, YOU'LL HAVE TO USE **TWO** PIECES

DIY HOME ALTERATION

NOW, DON'T FORGET THAT IN EUROPE THEY'RE 1 HOUR AHEAD OF US. SO, YOU'LL HAVE TO GO TO BED AN HOUR EARLIER AND SLEEP ON THE RIGHT

DAILY SMUT
SANTA STRIKE SENSATION
Pickets in Toyland

DRINGGGGGGG

THIS MEANS YOU WILL HAVE AN EXTRA HOUR IN BED, TO DO WHATEVER YOU NORMALLY DO.

ONLY FOR LONGER.
AND SOONER.

SO, **HAPPY EURO-CHRISTMAS**

AND **GOODNIGHT!**

SCIENCE OR SORCERY?

Eric T. Budge explains the 'wizardry' of TV transmission

1. Television pictures involve 3 main pieces of equipment — a camera, a transmitter and a receiver.

2. Let's suppose that there is a copy of the Two Ronnies Annual on the TV studio set. The camera picks up the light from the book and small mirrors inside the camera split this light up into 3 colour beams — blue, green and red — the 3 primary colours that make up any coloured light.

3. Then, as you can see, these 3 beams enter 3 tubes at the back of the camera. There the beams of light are changed into electric charges by a material sensitive to light. And the charges are changed into signals (or pulses) by an electron beam at the far end of each tube.
The signals then travel through cables into an adder and an encoder.

4. Notice that the adder has changed one set of colour signals into a black (and white) signal, while the encoder simply boosts the strength of the colour signals.

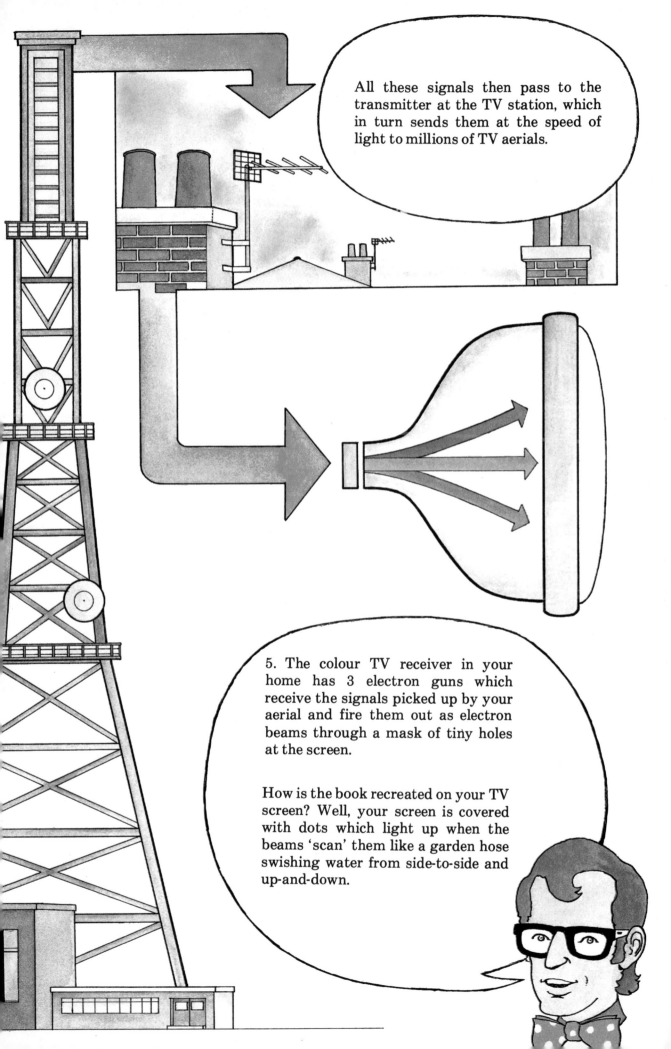

All these signals then pass to the transmitter at the TV station, which in turn sends them at the speed of light to millions of TV aerials.

5. The colour TV receiver in your home has 3 electron guns which receive the signals picked up by your aerial and fire them out as electron beams through a mask of tiny holes at the screen.

How is the book recreated on your TV screen? Well, your screen is covered with dots which light up when the beams 'scan' them like a garden hose swishing water from side-to-side and up-and-down.

So you wanna be a comedy Star

PALLADIUM

49. You are found whistling in the dressing room on the eve of the Palladium Show. Miss a turn.

36. Invited to appear on Eamonn Andrews' chat show. Return to Hospital.

York

38. Appear on the Tommy Cooper show. Advance five squares, just like that!

Mid

Hospital

Cleethorpes

32. You slip on a banana skin playing Bottom in A Midsummer Night's Dream. Advance to Hospital.

Batley

20. Meet the Ronnies on Jim'll Fix It. Advance 10 squares.

Bourne-mouth

17. Caught stealing Danny La Rue's wig while understudying Panto Dame. Go to Cop Shop.

Cop Shop

Pontrhydyfen

13. Described by critic as having no talent at all. Advance 5 squares.

RULES OF THE GAME

YOU NEED a dice and as many counters (or buttons) as players (4 players maximum)

WHO STARTS depends on the highest first roll of the dice. Thereafter each player takes alternate rolls unless a six is rolled which earns an extra go. If a player lands on another player he misses a go.

TO WIN a player must roll the exact number to get to the Palladium.

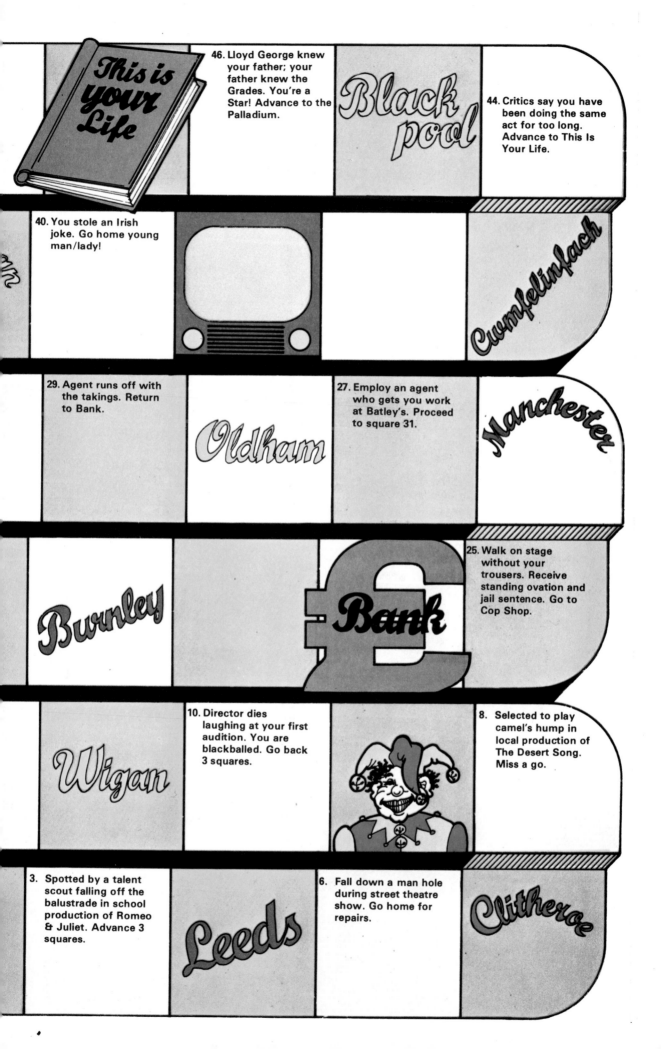

This is your Life

46. Lloyd George knew your father; your father knew the Grades. You're a Star! Advance to the Palladium.

Black pool

44. Critics say you have been doing the same act for too long. Advance to This Is Your Life.

40. You stole an Irish joke. Go home young man/lady!

Cwmfelinfach

29. Agent runs off with the takings. Return to Bank.

Oldham

27. Employ an agent who gets you work at Batley's. Proceed to square 31.

Manchester

Burnley

Bank

25. Walk on stage without your trousers. Receive standing ovation and jail sentence. Go to Cop Shop.

Wigan

10. Director dies laughing at your first audition. You are blackballed. Go back 3 squares.

8. Selected to play camel's hump in local production of The Desert Song. Miss a go.

3. Spotted by a talent scout falling off the balustrade in school production of Romeo & Juliet. Advance 3 squares.

Leeds

6. Fall down a man hole during street theatre show. Go home for repairs.

Clitheroe

the Two Ronnies
p that of any other
ow. With the help of
riters we have
ple of the News
s and Monologues.
he best is left to the
show — the
you can enjoy just a
xy of characters the
so superbly re-created.
emember a tune or

9 o'CLOCK NEWT

Have you noticed how politicians leave us alone over Christmas? Despite all evidence to the contrary it's not because the world stops turning in Christmas week. No, it seems that a Christmastime politicians make the supreme effort of joining the rest of the human race in the party spirit. What follows could best be described as an after-the-party political broadcast . . .

Millions of viewers rose as one from their comfy chairs drawn magnetically to their 'off' buttons by a familiar drone . . .

"There now follows a Party Political Broadcast"

But, less usually, those millions remained poised over their sets as they witnessed (instead of the drab faceless wonders they have come to love and ignore) an M.P. (dressed in dinner jacket, bow tie verging on the vertical, a red rose hanging loosely from behind his ear, a dab of lipstick on one cheek) enter the set with studied steadiness . . .

As viewers backed away in wonderment, the Member appeared to take notice of a chair (put there for his convenience). Stumbling across it, he mumbled . . .

'Good evening.
I am not the person you expected to see here tonight.
Oh no. Actually, he . . . Sir Hector . . . Thing . . . has been unalaidably devoid — in Amsterdam . . .
terdam . . . terdam. And I have stepped into his breach as it were at very short indeed.
I've just come from a hell of a party . . . a hell of a party conference, where we thrashed out several important people, including no less a man than the shadow . . . of your smile . . . terdam . . . terdam . . .'

Viewers up and down the country began swaying to the gruff sing-song tones of our Member, and it looked for a moment that a National party might be formed! But in the nick of time the Member's mind appeared to cleanse itself, and he began again . . .

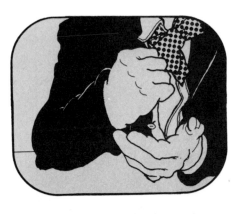

'Good evening. And I hope you're having one, and you are having one, tally ho!'

Before he could go further, a hand slid across the screen obliterating his slavering presence with a note which he interpreted thus:

'What Britain needs at this moment in our history is . . . "Scotch Broth 16p". But there are two sides to this,' *he continued turning the card over.* 'I've just been handed several letters which says, and I quote: "Pull yourself together. There's a nose behind your ear . . ."

'I think, in a sense, there's a nose behind everybody's ear,' *he continued, grabbing at the idea like a drowning man at a lifebelt.* 'And I'm not talking through the back of my neck when I say this. Isn't that the recipe for the ideal politician? A nose behind the ear? He can sniff the wind, listen to his nose, and of course smell his ear. Precisely. What? Some people may say, Oh yes it's easy for him to sit up there . . .' *As if to prove his point his elbows slipped downwards and his chin crunched into the table.* 'But you know,' *he concluded with ample evidence to support his case (if not his elbows),* 'It isn't!'

'Next,' *he threatened, wagging a finger or three,* 'Social hic-wality. I beg your pardon. Equality. Hic! Our position is and always has been . . .' *Searching for what his position might be, his hand wandered to his pocket and produced a lady's shoe.* 'There's a shoe in my pocket! And why not? What this country needs — and I'm speaking off the cuff *(indeed viewers could see him using his shirt cuff as a prompt card)* — is "Strict discipline. Rita. Evenings after six." *She'd* put Britain back on its feet. Europe! The G.C.E.! Are we to go round Europe tail in hand, cap between our legs? And what about Brussels? They're 18p now!'

The 'phone on his table began to ring . . .

'Ah! Room Service? I asked for two black coffees and the Daily Telegraph . . .'

At this point, mumbling something about leaving us with a thought, our Member mercifully ended it all by falling into a deep sleep!

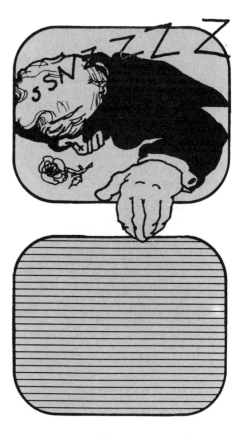

KID'S CALCU...

Modern technology has put your brain in your pocket in the shape of a pocket calculator, so watch where you sit. Here we show you how to have FUN with your pocket-sized brain. Below you will see a simple sketch which shows you everything you need to know about a calculator to play the games. So, by way of an introductory greeting —

1   Turn on your calculator
2   Press the decimal point
3   Press 7734
4   Turn the calculator upside down — and it's hello from us!

If you think of digits (1 or 2 or 3) as letters,.and numbers as words (345 is 'she' upside down on your calculator), what would be the code number for SHELL OIL? The answer is on the back page of the annual. How many other words can you make from digits?

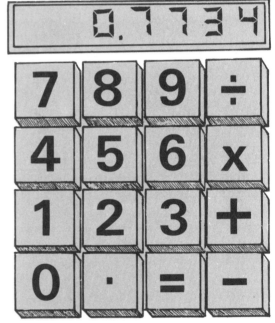

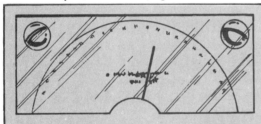

CURIOUSER AND CURIOUSER!

Can you find the swarm of eights?

9 x 9	+ 7 =
9 x 98	+ 6 =
9 x 987	+ 5 =
9 x 9876	+ 4 =
9 x 98765	+ 3 =
9 x 987654	+ 2 =
9 x 9876543	+ 1 =

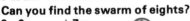

FIND THE MISSING NUMBER! (or the mystical 9)

a Ask a friend to write down in a line any number of digits (e.g. 857321). He must not let you see this number.

b Ask him to add all the digits together (i.e. 8+5+7+3+2+1 = 26)

c Ask him to subtract the result (i.e. 26) from his original line of digits (i.e. 857321 − 26 = 857295)

d Let him then strike out one digit from this new line (e.g. 857295) and ask him to tell you what number remains (i.e. 57295).

c By adding 5+7+2+9+5 (which equals 28) and subtracting that figure (i.e. 28) from the nearest multiple of 9 above it (i.e. 36 because 9 x 4 = 36) you will be able to tell him which number he struck out (because 36=28 = 8).

1TOR GAMES

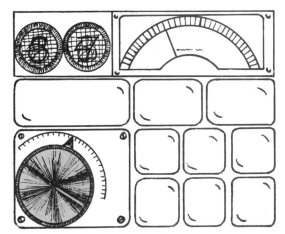

A SECRET REVEALED!

You can find out any person's age and the day and month on which the person was born by following these instructions:

Ask the person to write down the date and month on which he was born (if 23rd March then he will write down 233). He must multiply that figure by 2, add 5, multiply that result by 50, and add his actual age (if 30 he adds 30) and 365.

Ask him to hand this total to you. From it subtract 615 and you will have the date, month and age.

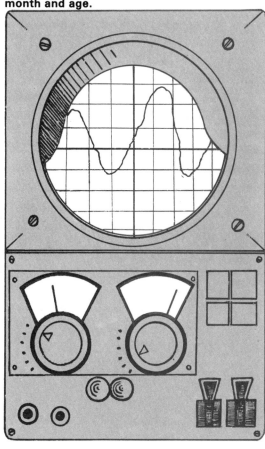

BAFFLE YOUR MOTHER AS TO HOW YOU KNOW HER AGE!

a Subtract your age from 99.
b Ask your mother to add the result of a to her age.
c Ask your mother to subtract 99 from the result of b.
d The result of c will always be the difference in your ages.
    So, add the result of c to your age.
e The result of d will be her age.

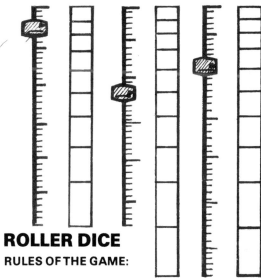

ROLLER DICE

RULES OF THE GAME:

1 2 or more people can play, 1 calculator per player and 2 dice is all you need.

2 Each player rolls the dice and the highest roll starts first, the lowest last. Thereafter each player rolls alternately.

3 Each player then rolls the dice again in turn and enters his or her roll on the calculators.

4 Each player rolls again and consults the instructions below to see what to do next.

5 After each player has rolled the dice ten times, the highest score is the WINNER!

INSTRUCTIONS:

If you roll a 2 then divide by 2

for a	3	multiply by 3
for a	4	enter nothing
for a	5	multiply by 5
for a	6	subtract 6
for a	7	add 7
for a	8	multiply by 8
for a	9	add 9
for a	10	enter nothing
for an	11	divide by 3
for a	12	multiply by 12

SYMBOLS

'Hello again. As you look at me you will notice two things. One, I'm very handsome, and two, there is a small rectangle at the bottom right-hand corner of your picture. This is a symbol which means that what you're watching is unsuitable for certain people. So if you're "certain people" — switch off!

'For the rest of you, let me explain what all our various symbols mean . . .

'This rectangle means you shouldn't watch the programme if you're offended by violence.

'*This* symbol means you shouldn't watch if you're offended by rectangles.

'*This* symbol means the programme coming up's going to be a bit naughty.

'*This* symbol means that we haven't given a warning but the programme's going to be naughty just the same so you'll get a nasty shock.

'*This* symbol means absolutely nothing but it was very expensive so we've got to use it. Either that or you're sitting there watching a very old egg.

'And this symbol means there's a squashed fly on our camera. But it's not as simple as that.

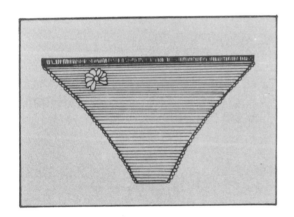

'*This* symbol tells us a programme will mention the word "Knickers".

For those who are offended by the knickers symbol itself, we've got this one:

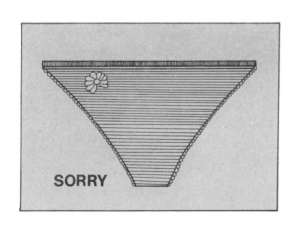

'But what about complaints? I'll just pull the knickers down a bit . . . there.

Now this symbol —

means Mary Whitehouse has phoned, whereas this one —

means she's beside herself. But we'll also use initials. This —

means the programme will include bare bottoms. This —

means curvaceous thighs,

and this —

V

means violence, so if the programme's got the lot you get:

BBC TV

'But this —

BBC

only means B.B.C. unless it's the other way up.

when it stands for a programme about a bald headed man dreaming of two well-developed ladies.

'Lastly to save money, we'll use road signs wherever possible:—

means you can only watch the programme if you're over thirty. This sign

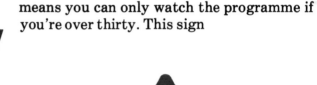

means the next programme's gardening club — or possibly David Attenborough in pursuit of the elephant. This one —

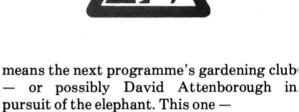

would tell you it was going to be the Rolling Stones and you'd get this

for a programme on family planning.

would be William Tell   would be William Don't Tell.

While this is quite clearly the very last episode of Z Cars. And guess what this would be—?

Yes, Father Dear Father.
And when anyone goes on too long you'll get this

CRIME and the COURTS

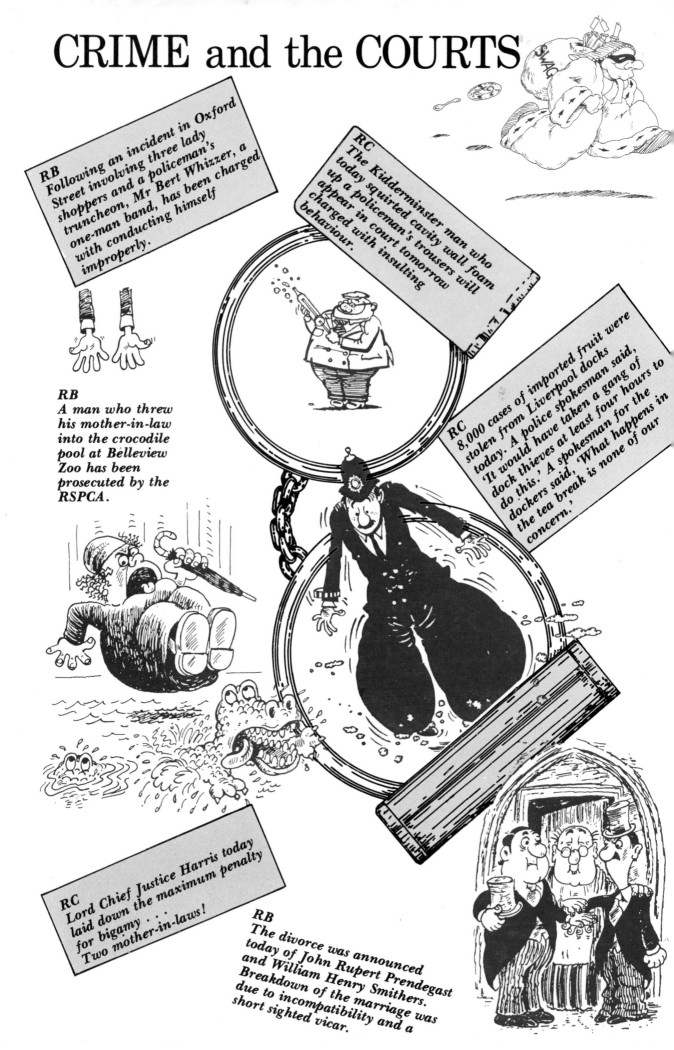

RB
Following an incident in Oxford Street involving three lady shoppers and a policeman's truncheon, Mr Bert Whizzer, a one-man band, has been charged with conducting himself improperly.

RC
The Kidderminster man who today squirted cavity wall foam up a policeman's trousers will appear in court tomorrow charged with insulting behaviour.

RB
A man who threw his mother-in-law into the crocodile pool at Belleview Zoo has been prosecuted by the RSPCA.

RC
8,000 cases of imported fruit were stolen from Liverpool docks today. A police spokesman said, 'It would have taken a gang of dock thieves at least four hours to do this.' A spokesman for the dockers said, 'What happens in the tea break is none of our concern.'

RC
Lord Chief Justice Harris today laid down the maximum penalty for bigamy . . . Two mother-in-laws!

RB
The divorce was announced today of John Rupert Prendegast and William Henry Smithers. Breakdown of the marriage was due to incompatibility and a short sighted vicar.

INDUSTRY

RB
Figures released today show that two out of every ten men work for a nationalised industry. While the other eight sit and watch them.

RC
Later in our series, (Meet the Workers), we'll talk to an East End docker who has retired after forty years to take a well-earned job.

RB
Then we'll interview the lady family planning officer who had triplets this week-end and was sacked for failing to report an accident.

RB
Tremendous results have been achieved by a team of British scientists who made ten laboratory rats smoke twenty cigarettes a day for a whole year. For this the team has been awarded the Nobel Prize — and the rats have got a colour telly with the coupons.

RB
Agriculture. Mr. Ernest Waldron, a cattle expert who's spent his whole life examining the back legs of cows, was given a special award today. Said Mr. Waldron, 'This is not the first time I've had a pat on the back.'

RC
The annual London Health and Beauty contest was won today by Miss Wapping. Second was Miss Not-Quite-So-Wapping, and third was Miss Absolutely-Piffling.

RC
Here's a piece of news. Mr Arthur Perkiss, the man who this week won £500,000 on the pools, has announced that he will never work another day in his life. So he's staying with British Rail.

DAILY INFLATION

now ~~6p~~ 8p!!

MINISTER SPEAKS!

When it comes to discussing serious issues of economy and high finance, our Minister of Inflation has a way of getting to the heart of the problem as it really affects 'the man in, the streets' . . .

'I'm the Minister of Inflation. Now, what *is* inflation?'

'Look at this graph . . .

'It shows the cost of spending a penny at Euston Station every year since 1884. No mean feat in itself. As you can see it's getting very expensive, but the most important point on the graph is point A.

'Why? Because I can hang my umbrella on it . . . Thus!'

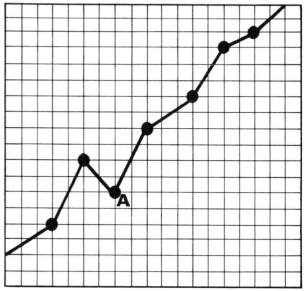

'What about prices? Trousers for example.

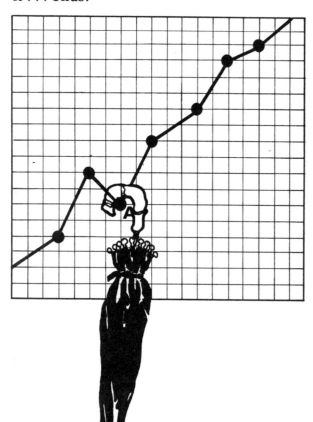

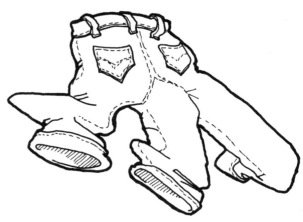

What do we notice? Well firstly they've got three legs but that's just to be on the safe side. Unless you live on the Kings Road, in which case there's no safe side! Now, trousers *are* going up alarmingly. And the question is, what does this give us besides a pain in the crotch? And what about skirts. If we look up skirts we see they're going up even faster than trousers!'

'The trouble is, you see, the pound is no longer worth the paper it's printed on. By 1984 paper hankies will be six pounds each so it'll be cheaper to blow your nose on a fiver.

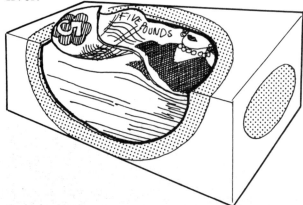

'So, we in the Government are introducing a system known as barter. It does away with your money, something we've been working at for years.'

WHAT ABOUT VAT?

RHUBARB!

'When they say, "What about V.A.T.?" I'll say, "Rhubarb!"'

'Take my wife. She's worth a cow and a sheep. My mother-in-law? Just a cow. They could buy each othe and I'd be left with a sheep. Then I could put the sheep on a horse and win a thousand hamsters in the two thousand guinea pigs.

'However, I've suggested an even simpler system and the Chancellor of the Exchequer has given his full support (though what it's full of I can't tell you). My plan is to replace money with dogs.

Here is a rough example —

Here is a smooth example —
'The system is decimal. Ten poms to a poodle, ten poodles in a piddle and a hundred dog pees in the dog pound . . .

'Just yesterday at Christies a Constable went for a Great Dane and a Great Dane went for a postman — so there you have it!

'If you send for our government pamphlet on inflation I'll slip in a very nice picture of my secretary Miss Rita Crampett. Five pounds should cover it. On the other hand she's a big girl, so make it a tenner.'

SPECIAL OFFER!

£££££s!!

But Now, Here's the Late News...

RB
There was an accident involving Britain's worst goalkeeper, Bill Berkley, who has already let through 157 goals this season. Shouting out, I'm a complete failure Berkley threw himself in front of a bus . . . Luckily the bus passed under him and he wasn't hurt

RC
At the Royal Air Show today, Luigi Bregnozi, the famous Italian drunken air ace, was not permitted to do his celebrated dive through the sound barrier. The controller said he could not endanger the crowd with a high tiddley iteye boom boom!

RB
A survey on the decline of morals in Britain reveals that in Liverpool alone on each day last week an average of 267 women made love to an unmarried man. The man is now recovering in hospital.

RC
The World Masochism Centre opened today in Edmonton. There are huge illuminated signs all over it telling you all about the wonderful things inside, but no door.

RB
Reports are coming in that aboriginals in the remotest part of Sarawak are having their first taste of Christianity. He was the Reverend J. G. Podmore of Warminster.

RB
In support of their salary claim, the Irish Wall of Death Riders' Association starts a go-slow today.

RC
Finally, here is a police message. Will the man who lost eight bottles of whisky at Euston station this morning please go to the Lost Property office by Platform Nine where the man who found them has just been handed in.

RB
And some more late items of news. Her Majesty the Queen went on a short informal walkabout today after she hit her thumb with a hammer.

RC
Whilst at Hickstead today, Princess Anne had three clear rounds and was then asked to leave by the landlord.

RC
Mr. Osbert Grove, Britain's worst ever postman, who claims he was wrongfully dismissed by the GPO, today delivered a petition to the Queen — at 15 Station Street, Scunthorpe.

RB
Well, that's all for this week. Next week I'll be reviewing a book that's just become a best seller in Scotland, entitled Indoor Games for Flag Days.

RC
Then we'll have hints on coarse fishing . . . followed by lewd hockey, suggestive cricket and obscene golf.

"So it's Goodnight from me..."
"...And it's Goodnight from him."

SOLUTIONS TO TRICKS & PUZZLES

1. If you compare the illustration below with the original 5-square diagram you will see which 3 picks you should have moved.

2. Well was it simpler? The 8 picks have been removed leaving only 2 squares on the table.

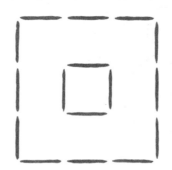

3. The 10-pointed star becomes a 5-pointed star if you let a little water fall into the very centre of the first shape. Before your very eyes it will become a star with only 5 points.

4. To make the coin fall into the bottle without touching it, let a drop of water fall upon the bent middle of the pick. See? Easy when you know how.

5. The illustration shows how the 3-pick bridge is built.